YOUR WILLY

AN OWNER'S MANUAL

By Martin Baxendale

MODELS COVERED BY THIS MANUAL

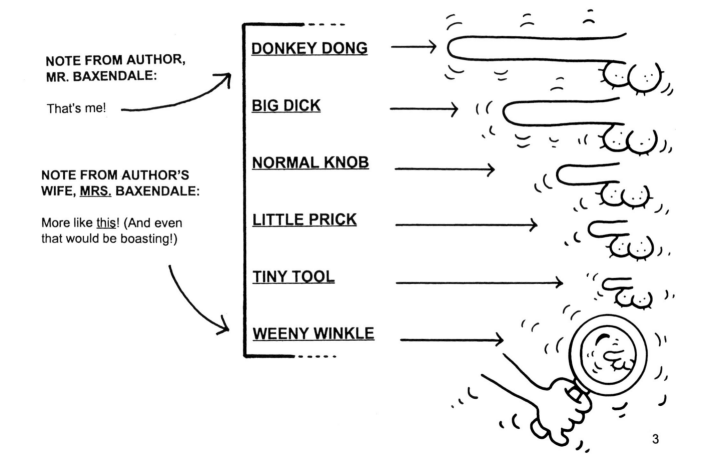

BASIC FEATURES

AUTHOR'S NOTE:
I have decided to use my <u>own</u> Willy as an example here. Please don't be embarrassed if <u>your</u> Willy doesn't measure up to mine; I am, after all, exceptionally well endowed.

Amazing horse-like throbbing length.

Balls like a prize bull.

Goes like a sewing machine, with the staying-power of a North Sea oil drill.

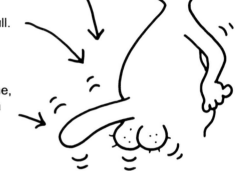

(Apologies to any female readers who may have now fainted).

EDITOR'S NOTE:
And here is <u>Mrs.</u> Baxendale's version.

Very short, droopy dribbly bit.

Dangly sweaty bits.

Wrinkly, sagging scrotum.

Varicose vein.

Pubic hairs going grey and falling out with age.

Smelly feet.

ROUTINE MAINTENANCE

Your Willy is a high-performance unit which requires regular care and attention. We strongly recommend that you carry out the following routine maintenance procedures at least every fifteen minutes throughout the day, no matter where you are.

1) Insert hand in pocket and locate Willy.

2) Adjust Willy position from left to right or vice versa.

3) Jiggle balls about a bit.

4) Scratch scrotum.

5) Remove hand from pocket and sniff fingers.

5

STORAGE WHEN NOT IN USE

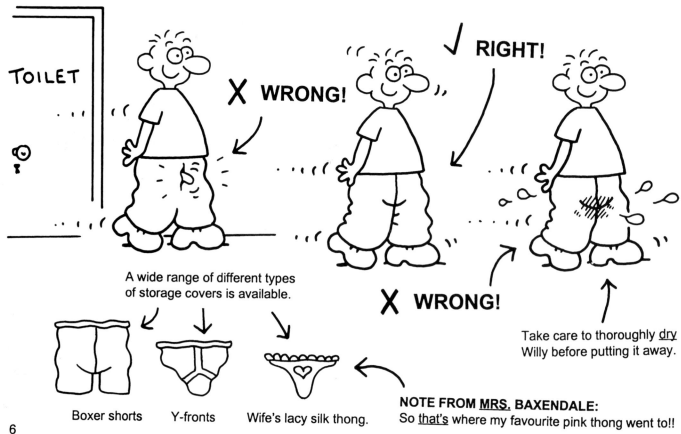

TOILET

X WRONG!

✓ RIGHT!

X WRONG!

A wide range of different types of storage covers is available.

Take care to thoroughly <u>dry</u> Willy before putting it away.

Boxer shorts

Y-fronts

Wife's lacy silk thong.

NOTE FROM <u>MRS.</u> BAXENDALE:
So <u>that's</u> where my favourite pink thong went to!!

YOUR WILLY IN SEX MODE

This is of course the most popular operating mode, although Weeing Mode (see page 22) can come a very close second if you're really, really bursting.

This basic operating guide should prove especially useful to less experienced Willy owners, and a helpful refresher course for older hands.

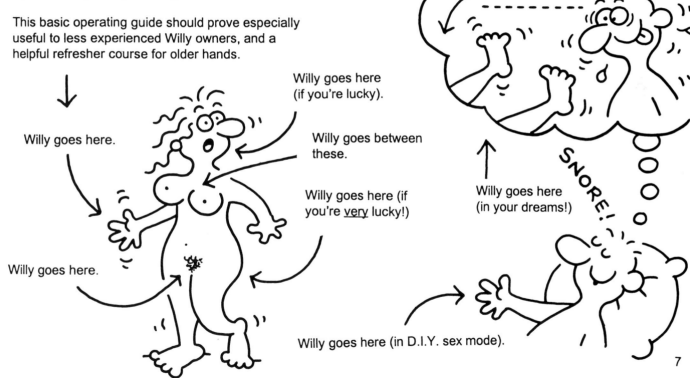

Willy goes here.

Willy goes here.

Willy goes here.

Willy goes here (if you're lucky).

Willy goes between these.

Willy goes here (if you're very lucky!)

(Write the name of your favourite sexy pop star here).

Willy goes here (in your dreams!)

SNORE!

Willy goes here (in D.I.Y. sex mode).

Willy does **not** go up nose or in ear (trust me, I've tried).
Willy does **not** go in here (unless you want to end up in Casualty, like I did).
Your partner's sister.
Your partner's best friend.
Any other fit birds.
SUCK!
SUCK!
SUCK!
HOOVER
VROOM!!
VROOM!!
If you're with a long-term partner (like the lovely Mrs. Baxendale) your Willy does **not** go anywhere near any of them (unless you want to end up in Casualty, like I did - a number of times!)

NOTE FROM THE PUBLISHER:

As a raging queen myself, and proud of it, I was outraged to find that the author, Mr. Baxendale, had assumed in the previous two pages that all Willy owners are heterosexual and have <u>female</u> partners!!!

To put things right, I have instructed Mr. Baxendale to include on this page a cut-out-and-glue kit to allow <u>gay</u> Willy owners like myself to adapt the female partner illustrated on page 7 into a more suitable <u>male</u> partner.

Freddy Mercury moustache.

Hairy chest.

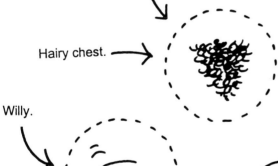

Gold medallion.

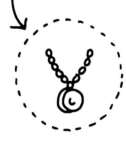

Willy.

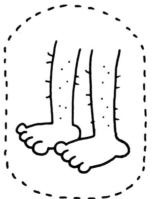

Hairy legs.

<u>WHEN</u> TO USE YOUR WILLY IN SEX MODE:

Do try to remember that there are times when inconsiderately trying to operate your Willy in sex mode may cause your partner considerable nuisance and annoyance.

Persistently and thoughtlessly attempting sex mode operation at such moments may even result in serious damage to the Willy and its associated bits and bobs (<u>Mrs.</u> Baxendale always keeps a large pair of nutcrackers by the bed for just such occasions).

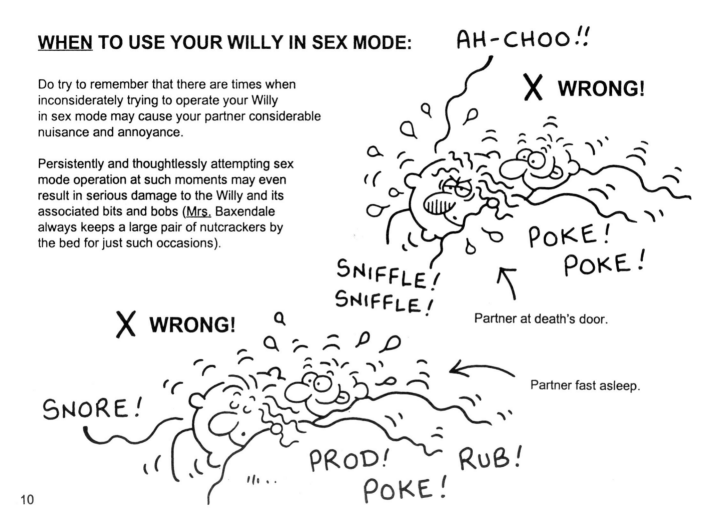

Partner at death's door.

Partner fast asleep.

With experience and practice, you should find that your ability to read the signals and tell when it's okay to use your Willy in sex mode will improve.

As a general guide for less experienced Willy owners, it usually goes something like this (at least it does in our house)....

Last 20 minutes of World Cup final...England 3, Germany 3.

WHERE TO USE YOUR WILLY IN SEX MODE:

Of course, the bedroom isn't the only place you can use your Willy in sex mode. More adventurous owners will want to try a wide range of different situations.

Outdoors is very popular; in the garden, out in the countryside, public parks etc. But don't get too carried away....

✓ **RIGHT!**   In the bushes.

BOUNCE!
BOUNCE!

✗ **WRONG!**   ← Waiting for a bus.

13

USING WILLY WITH <u>MULTIPLE PARTNERS</u>:

SERIOUS HAZARD WARNING!!!
We really cannot stress too much how dangerous it can be to attempt Willy sex mode operation with more than one partner at a time (especially if you're in a long-term relationship).

Less experienced Willy owners in particular please note: This may result in very serious (and possibly irreparable) damage to your Willy.

THERE HE IS !! GRAB THE TWO-TIMING BASTARD !!

GET HIS TROUSERS OFF! I'LL FETCH THE GARDEN SHEARS !!

And even in the case of a sex mode threesome where you and your partner <u>agree</u>, do bear in mind that she may not have quite the same thing in mind as <u>you</u> do.

14

MAKING YOUR "PACKAGE" LOOK BIGGER:

Many Willy owners like to make their "package" look a little bigger and more eye-catching when trying to impress girls at the beach or the poolside.

The traditional standby has always been the rolled-up sock down the trunks. But do take care to use a <u>clean</u> sock. The stench of smelly sock wafting up from your crotch area isn't a great come-on, as I found to my cost one hot afternoon at the beach last summer.

Likewise, a beach-towel down your trunks is probably overdoing it a bit (when I tried that one, I was told to leave the beach and seek immediate medical attention).

And though an ice-cream cone down your trunks might seem a good idea if you really want to impress the girls (as I thought one day at Bognor) with hindsight, I should probably have finished the ice-cream first.

X WRONG!

Beach towel down trunks.

X WRONG!

Ice cream cone down trunks.

WILLY ADD-ON ATTACHMENTS:

There are various add-on attachments available that can enhance the basic performance of your Willy unit in sex mode operation.

But do take care to buy them from reputable suppliers and don't be tempted to save money by making them yourself, as I tried to do.

My home-made <u>Willy extension</u>, for example, was a total disaster.

With all the violent bashing around during use, the plasticine extension unfortunately re-modelled itself and came out at the end looking like my uncle Bert - which gave <u>Mrs.</u> Baxendale a bit of a shock, I can tell you (and has given me a few unpleasant nightmares too).

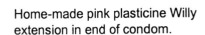

Home-made pink plasticine Willy extension in end of condom.

In addition to Willy extensions, you can also purchase various performance enhancing tickling and vibrating add-on attachments.

Here again, it's not advisable to skimp but to buy the best you can find. My own D.I.Y. attempt with a nail-brush for a clit-tickler and an electric shaver for a vibrator attachment, all held on to my Willy with rubber bands, went horribly, horribly wrong.

Mrs. Baxendale couldn't sit down for a week afterwards. And to this day she still claims it was a deliberate ploy to sneakily give her a "shaven haven" for my own perverse pleasure.

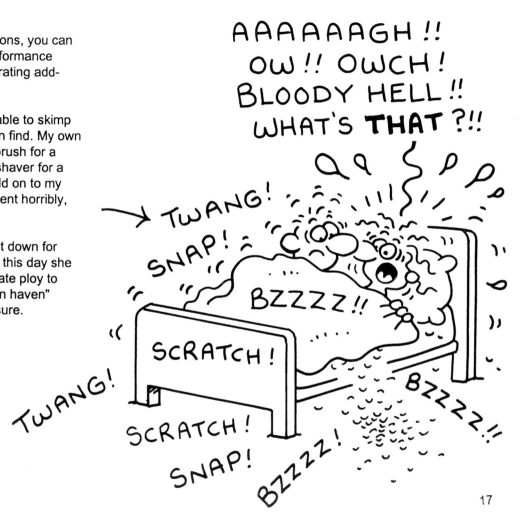

17

THE EMBARRASSING PUBLIC STIFFY:

Getting an enormous trouser-stretching tent-pole of a stiffy at the wrong time and the wrong place - during a business meeting, squashed against strangers on a crowded train, lying in the dentist's chair (white uniforms turn me on...and the drill vibrations, oh man!) - can be excruciatingly embarrassing.

Of course you can always try to hide it, but eventually you'll have to stand up, come out from behind the office water cooler, put down that porno mag - so the important thing is to try to make it go away as quickly as possible.

Your best bet is to think about someone or something incredibly unsexy, ugly and repulsive. That usually does the trick (although not always, I have to admit, for <u>me</u>).

HOW TO <u>KEEP GOING</u> IN SEX MODE:

<u>Finishing</u> too soon in sex mode is a common problem which can leave your partner unsatisfied, grumpy and (in Mrs. Baxendale's case) even downright violent.

But this is also easily solved by thinking of someone or something very ugly and unsexy, to help you last longer until your partner has been fully satisfied and (in Mrs. Baxendale's case) put down the nutcrackers.

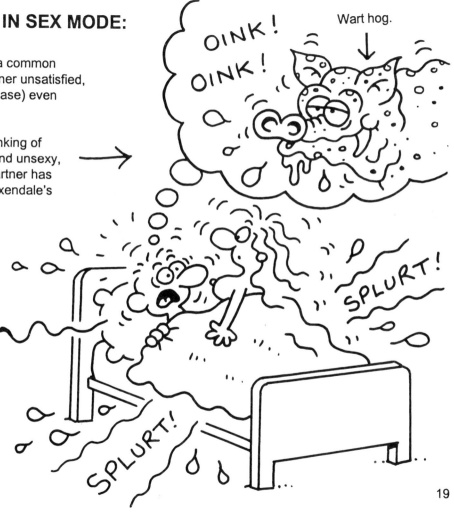

IF YOUR WILLY <u>FAILS TO WORK</u> IN SEX MODE:

AUTHOR'S NOTE:
Sorry, can't help you here. It's never happened to me!

AUTHOR'S WIFE'S NOTE:
Here are some scenes from a typical night in the Baxendale household, which amply illustrate the most common cause of Willy failure in sex mode and how to avoid it:

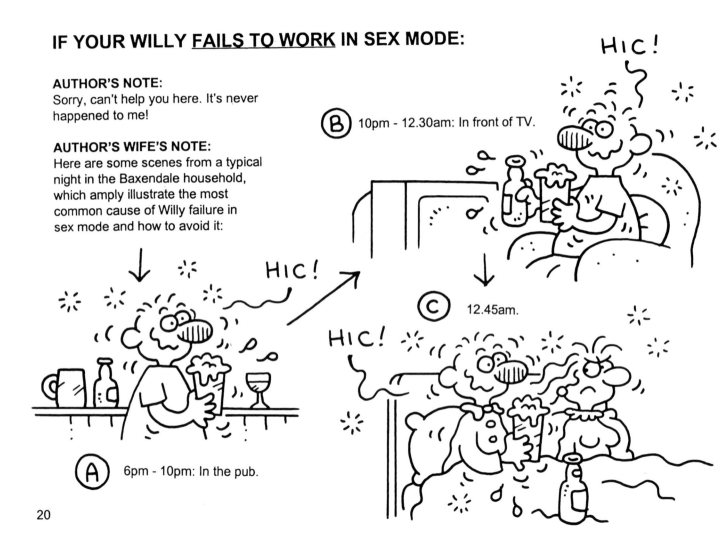

(A) 6pm - 10pm: In the pub.

(B) 10pm - 12.30am: In front of TV.

(C) 12.45am.

AUTHOR'S NOTE:
Oh that's <u>very</u> nice! Thank you <u>so</u> much, darling!!

Well, then <u>here</u> is my tip for getting your Willy <u>going</u> <u>again</u> if you're having problems in sex mode:

Just imagine your favourite sexy pop stars <u>wrestling</u> <u>in</u> <u>jelly</u>. Always works for me - in fact I often think about it during sex even when I'm <u>not</u> having any problems!!

AUTHOR'S WIFE'S NOTE:
Oh yeah? Well <u>I</u> imagine you're Tom Cruise! So there!! Now where did I put those nutcrackers?

21

YOUR WILLY IN WEEING MODE

The trouble with a Willy in weeing mode is its complete and utter lack of anything even resembling an accurate aim - at least in the hands of the typical male operative.

Driven to distraction by my own impersonations of a garden sprinkler, <u>Mrs.</u> Baxendale designed this toilet adaptor for me, which we have patented and will shortly be marketing at a very reasonable price:

Extra-wide bowl adaptor makes a larger target.

Wrap-around perspex splash guard.

SUCK!

BLOW

Absorbent sponge toilet 'seat' soaks up drips and dribbles (simply squeeze out into bowl after use).

Extractor fan sucks-in stray sprinkles and squirts.

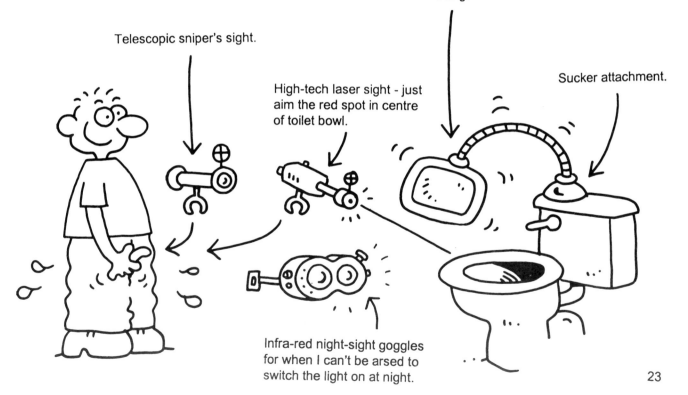

And here are some other ideas Mrs. Baxendale has tried, to get me to improve my aim in the toilet. You might like to try them too.

Telescopic sniper's sight.

High-tech laser sight - just aim the red spot in centre of toilet bowl.

Extra-large magnifying reading glass to help me see what I'm doing.

Sucker attachment.

Infra-red night-sight goggles for when I can't be arsed to switch the light on at night.

23

Of course there are times when you can't get to the toilet, e.g. when there's a huge queue for the bathroom at a party, and you have to improvise.

Best choice at parties is usually the garden (since there's generally too many people hanging around near the punch bowl).

But a handy tip is to look around for a hosepipe first. Held at the right angle, alongside your willy, it'll look like you're thoughtfully watering your host's roses for him, rather than pissing on his petunias, should he spot you from the house.

Or you can stick the hosepipe up your bum, lie on your back in the middle of the lawn and pretend to be a sprinkler....although I <u>was</u> asked to leave and never come back after that particular trick, as it was a Sunday afternoon garden party (but in my defence, I was very, very, very drunk).

DRUNKEN WEEING MODE:

Speaking of weeing when drunk, this is when most Willy owners are at their most <u>unpredictable</u> as well as their most inaccurate.

Not only does their aim and sense of direction become virtually non-existent, but they become quite incapable of telling the difference between a lavatory and (for example) a wardrobe.

Your never know <u>where</u> they might decide to wee in their alcohol-befuddled state, which is why <u>Mrs.</u> Baxendale likes to play safe when she knows I'm going to get rat-arsed, and takes various precautions that you may also find useful:

Cling-film over goldfish bowl.

Umbrella over favourite pot plant.

AAAAGH!!!

PSSSS!

BOING!!

Scary clown puppet to stop me trying to wee in the wardrobe.

25

IF YOUR WILLY <u>FAILS TO WORK</u> IN WEEING MODE:

This sometimes happens to Willy owners when trying to wee in a public toilet surrounded by strangers - you suddenly find you just can't go, no matter how hard you try.

Talk about embarrassing! After a few minutes of trying and trying without so much as a dribble, you eventually start to look like someone who likes hanging around in public toilets holding his Willy, instead of a genuine weeing toilet user.

And as more and more people stare and glare at you, the worse it gets - although the sheer panic and terror as they start to hit and kick you does, I find, eventually help to get the required flow going.

I carry these basic weeing aids with me at all times, just for this sort of eventuality.

SWOOSH !!

Walkman with mix tape featuring the sounds of waterfalls, pouring rain, dripping taps, showers, fountains, etc.

Thermos of iced water for dipping fingers into.

Picture postcard of seaside with lots of cold seawater and waves.

AVOIDING WILLY ACCIDENTS

The commonest Willy accident is of course the Willy-caught-in-trouser-zip horror that so many of us have experienced at one time or another.

But there are other, even more horrifying, potential accidents just waiting to happen to careless Willy owners. Here are a few especially dangerous situations that all Willy owners should take great care to avoid (I certainly won't be trying any of these again!)

Playing with kittens in the nude.

Ironing in the nude.

HAVING FUN WITH YOUR WILLY

Apart from sex mode (obviously) there's all kinds of fun you can have with your Willy. Here are a couple of my personal favourites.

A) Cheer up a wet Sunday morning by tucking your Willy and balls between your legs, slipping into your partner's bra, and prancing around the bedroom pretending to be a girlie.

Then turn round, bend over, point to your Willy and balls sticking out beneath your bum cheeks, and say: "Look!!! Worst case of piles in medical history!"

That one always gets a big laugh from <u>Mrs.</u> Baxendale.

NOTE FROM <u>MRS.</u> BAXENDALE: No it bloody doesn't!! For God's sake, grow up you pathetic excuse for a man!!!

29

B) My favourite drunken party trick. This always has our dinner party guests screaming with laughter.

Me throwing my voice (those evening classes in ventriloquism were worth every penny!)

WHERE'S THE TOILET?

Spectacles on my Willy.

This trick is also useful if you want to sunbathe nude in the garden or at the beach, but are worried about neighbours or passers-by spotting you naked Willy.

Simply add some sun-glasses, false moustache and a cigarette (not lit!) and people won't think your Willy is on view but that you're sunbathing with a very small man between your legs (so no embarrassing moments if strangers stroll past or neighbours stop to chat over the fence).

NOTE FROM MRS. BAXENDALE:
For God's sake, someone please shoot him!!! I'll pay good money!

MAKING THINGS WITH YOUR WILLY

Unfortunately there aren't actually that many things you can <u>make</u> with your Willy - apart from pretty patterns in the snow if you're artistic and have a steady hand (I went one step further last winter and tried making an <u>ice</u> <u>sculpture</u> with mine but ended up in hospital for two weeks with frost bite).

However, if you really want to, you can always make one of <u>these</u>; it's usually not too difficult, even for a beginner. They're quite cute, and twins make excellent book ends.

But do try not to get too carried away.

WAIL!

KICK!

31